Writing
Dystopian Fiction
A Brainstorming Guide

Funny Face Fiction LTD.

Writing Dystopian Fiction: A Brainstorming Guide
Copyright © Funny Face Fiction

All Rights Reserved

First edition
ebook ISBN: 978-1-990631-33-7
Print ISBN: 978-1-990631-50-4
Published by Funny Face Fiction Ltd.
Please visit us at www.funnyfacefiction.com

Table of Contents

"

I think it's fascinating to look at a world that an author has created that has sort of stemmed from the world now, and usually dystopian books point out something about our current world and exaggerates a tendency or a belief.

Veronica Roth

Introduction

Hey there, writers! If you've ever been intrigued by worlds of darkness, oppression, and gripping tales of survival, you're in for an exciting journey. In this guide, we are diving into brainstorming dystopian fiction.

Specifically, the things you need to think about when you are writing your book. So, grab your pens and imagination, and let's get started!

According to Merriam Webster, they define Dystopian as: *of, relating to, or being an imagined world or society in which people lead dehumanized, fearful lives: relating to or characteristic of a dystopia.*

Dystopian fiction takes us into often grim and not-so-distant futures, where society has usually taken a turn for the worse. In these stories, you'll find worlds twisted by oppressive governments, environmental disasters, or extreme technological control.

They make us think, "What if our world ended up like this?"

These tales are more than just gloomy predictions; they challenge us to consider big questions about humanity, freedom, and the fine line between order and chaos.

Dystopian novels aren't just about dark scenarios; they're about resilience, hope, a sense of community and the strength of characters facing tough odds. They're a mirror reflecting our deepest fears and a window into how we might overcome them.

WRITING DYSTOPIAN

Imagine a world where society has taken a dark turn. Dystopian fiction paints this kind of future. It's a genre where stories unfold in a future world marred by control, fear, and loss of freedom.

Think of well-known stories like The Hunger Games, Brave New World, Divergent or 1984.

These stories exhibit advanced technology, the struggle for freedom, and a society governed by oppression.

Creating the Dystopian World

Building the stage is crucial. Your dystopian world needs life, history, and rules that make it believable. Describe the society's customs, geography, and traditions.

Ask yourself:
How did it get this way?
What events led to this future?

The more vibrant and realistic your world is, the easier it is for readers to get lost in your pages.

Developing Characters

Characters are the heart of your story. Make them relatable by giving them fears, desires, and personalities that mirror the challenges of the dystopian world.

Think about what motivates them to act in this harsh reality. Remember, characters are the bridge that connects readers to your story's emotions.

Defining the Conflict

Every story thrives on conflict, and in dystopian fiction, it's a battle against the world itself. Whether it's an individual standing against society or a fight for survival, this central conflict drives the narrative. Make it intense, emotional, and impossible to look away from.

Crafting the Plot

Structure is your friend. Start with introducing the dystopian world, then present the protagonist and their struggles. Raise the stakes as the story progresses until they reach the thrilling climax. And don't forget the resolution—the outcome of the battle your characters have been fighting.

Themes and Messages
Dystopian fiction isn't just about futuristic settings; it's a platform to explore real-world issues. Themes like power, freedom, conformity, and human resilience can be woven into the story. Let your writing shine a light on these themes subtly, giving depth to your tale.

Building Tension and Atmosphere
Creating the right mood is essential. Use descriptions, setting details, and pacing to build tension and an eerie atmosphere. Readers should feel the weight of the world the characters live in, making their experiences even more immersive.

Writing Dialogue
Dialogue brings characters to life. Craft conversations that reveal personalities, motivations, and relationships. Make it sound authentic, like real people talking, even in an unreal world.

Overcoming Writer's Block
Stuck? It happens to all writers. Take breaks, explore new ideas, or draw inspiration from the world around you. Writer's block is just a temporary roadblock; you'll find a way around it.

Editing and Revising
The first draft is just the beginning. Polish the story by revising and editing. Check for consistency, clarity, and grammar. Don't shy away from feedback; it's the key to making your story the best it can be.

World Ending

Scenarios

One of the first things to do is decide how your world became dystopian. Now there are a ton of ways that you can choose, and I've compiled a list of world-ending scenarios to help you decide what way works best for your story. There are also examples from novels, movies, and TV series that you are probably familiar with.

Alien Invasion
During an alien invasion, extraterrestrial forces arrive and impose their rule. Most times, the aliens are more technologically and scientifically advanced. Which gives them an unfair advantage.

This usually leads to a struggle for survival and resistance against a powerful new authority.

TV series: Falling Skies.
In this post-apocalyptic show, survivors unite to combat an Espheni alien invasion. A leader of the survivors is Tom Mason, a former history professor. His group confronts aliens, rebuilds society, forges alliances, and safeguards their families.

Novel/Movie: The 5th Wave (Rick Yancey)
This novel follows the story of Cassie Sullivan as she navigates a world devastated by alien attacks. These attacks happen in waves.

Anarchy

The more dissatisfaction people have with the existing laws, the more controversy brews like a storm. Once the seeds of dissent and upheaval take root, society turns down a path from which there is no return.

The emergence of anarchy, fuelled by the determination of a united group, serves as a powerful catalyst for societal change. But it is not always for the better.

Novel/Movie: The Postman (David Brin)
In a future America destroyed by war, a drifter finds an abandoned postal truck and starts delivering mail, bringing hope to survivors.

Novel/Movie: The Road (Cormac McCarthy)
This post-apocalyptic novel is all about a world in chaos, where it's every man for himself. A dad and his son fight tooth and nail to stay alive.

Artificial Intelligence Uprising

Self-aware AI systems rebel against human control, leading to a world where humans are subjugated by their own creations.

Movie: The Terminator series
The future has sent a cyborg assassin to eliminate Sarah Connor, mother of John Connor, the future resistance leader. Kyle Reese, a soldier from the same future, has the task of protecting Sarah and preventing the Terminator's mission.

Novel/Movie: I, Robot (Isaac Asimov)
This collection of short stories explores the interactions between humans and intelligent robots, delving into the ethical implications and potential consequences of AI becoming self-aware.

Asteroids

The cosmos can unleash its fury, and hurtle an errant asteroid towards us, igniting a cataclysmic explosion. Rockets launched, satellites strewn—these human intrusions into space might inadvertently trigger a domino effect, unleashing a cosmic cascade of havoc that reverberates across our fragile planet.

Movie: Armageddon
The government drafts a bunch of oil drillers.
They task them with travelling to an Earth-
threatening asteroid to drill into its surface
and plant a nuclear bomb to prevent a
catastrophic collision.

Novel: The Hammer of God (Arthur C.
Clarke)
In this novel, they discovered an asteroid to be
on a collision course with Earth, and
humanity races against time to develop a
solution to avert the disaster.

Biological Warfare
Genetic manipulation or engineered viruses lead to
catastrophic biological consequences, by decimating
populations and changing the world forever.
Biological warfare usually involves genetically
engineered pathogens that lead to pandemics, causing
mass casualties and societal breakdowns.

Novel: The Andromeda Strain (Michael
Crichton)
In this sci-fi thriller, scientists are studying a
dangerous alien microorganism that could kill
everyone on Earth.

Movie/TV Series: 12 Monkeys
In a dystopian future ravaged by a deadly
virus, a time traveller is sent back to the past
to uncover the origins of the pandemic and
prevent it.

Chemical Warfare

The exposure of chemicals to living things would certainly destroy most of the planet. Chemical agents are extremely dangerous synthetic chemicals. They can release them as a gas, liquid, or aerosol, or as agents attached to particles to become a powder.

Novel: The Poisonwood Bible (Barbara Kingsolver)
This story isn't your typical dystopian novel, but it delves into the unexpected fallout of chemical warfare in the Cold War era and how it affects a missionary family in Africa.

Movie: 28 Days Later
This horror movie is set in a post-apocalyptic world where a virus created through chemical experiments causes chaos in the UK.

Cultural Regression

Societies reject progress and revert to archaic norms and values, causing a decline in knowledge, technology, and freedom.

Novel/Movie/TV Series: The Handmaid's Tale (Margaret Atwood)
This series depicts a theocratic dystopia where cultural regression has led to the subjugation of women and losing personal freedoms.

Movie: Planet of the Apes
In this classic science fiction film, astronauts land on a planet where humans have devolved into primitive creatures, while intelligent apes have risen to dominance.

Drought
A long-term drought leads to widespread water
scarcity and crop failures, triggering conflicts over
dwindling resources. People must adapt to arid
landscapes and find new ways to secure water and
food.

Novel: Scorched (Theresa Shaver)
A prolonged drought and no more water
rations forces a family to follow an old map to
a promised risky journey south, following an
old map to a promised valley abundant with
water.

Novel: Dry (Neal Shusterman and
Jarrod Shusterman)
In this young adult novel, a prolonged drought
in California leads to chaos and desperation
as water becomes scarce and society unravels.

Earthquake (Natural Disaster)
Earthquakes and aftershocks can lead to destroyed
civilizations. Breakdowns of government and systems.
Families will be separated, medical emergencies will
multiply.

Movie: San Andreas
A devastating series of earthquakes along the
San Andreas Fault threatens the West Coast of
the United States, leading to widespread chaos
and destruction.

Novel: The Rift (Walter Jon Williams)
A massive earthquake in the American
Southwest leads to a series of catastrophic
events, including the formation of a new

inland sea, reshaping society in unexpected ways.

Ecological Collapse

An abrupt and extensive breakdown of ecosystems disrupts the food chain, causing widespread food shortages, famine, and societal collapse.

Movie: WALL-E
In this animated film, Earth has become uninhabitable because of environmental pollution and waste. This forces humans to live in space while a waste-collecting robot named WALL-E remains on Earth.

Movie: Interstellar
A science fiction movie portrays Earth confronting an ecological catastrophe due to crop failures and environmental degradation, sparking a quest to locate a new livable planet.

Economic Collapse

A global economic meltdown leads to widespread poverty, inequality, and social unrest, ultimately destabilizing governments and institutions.

Novel/Movie: The Children of Men (P.D. James)
Set in a future where global infertility has resulted in societal breakdown, the film depicts a world grappling with economic collapse, authoritarian rule, and a dwindling population.

Novel: The Mandibles: A Family (Lionel Shriver)
In this novel, the U.S. economy goes bust and a family fight for their lives.

EMP
An Electromagnetic Pulse (EMP) could cause widespread chaos, disrupting vital systems, and plunging societies into disarray.

Novel: One Second After (William R. Forstchen)
This novel depicts the aftermath of an EMP attack on the United States, resulting in the collapse of modern civilization and the struggles of a small town to survive.

TV Series: Revolution
They set this series in a world where all electronic devices and power sources have been disabled by a mysterious EMP-like event, leading to a post-apocalyptic landscape.

Environmental Collapse
Global climate change leads to extreme weather events, rising sea levels, and resource scarcity, causing societies to crumble.

Novel: The Windup Girl (Paolo Bacigalupi)
This biopunk novel is set in a future world where environmental degradation, climate change, and biotechnology have caused societal collapse and environmental catastrophe.

TV Series: Years and Years
This drama series explores a near-future
world grappling with environmental collapse,
political instability, and societal breakdown as
climate change and environmental disasters
escalate.

Flood
A rapid rise in sea levels, often caused by melting ice caps or catastrophic weather events, results in widespread flooding, displacing populations and causing resource shortages.

Movie: Waterworld
In this post-apocalyptic film, the polar ice caps
have melted, submerging most of Earth's
landmasses and leading to a world covered in
water.

Novel: The Drowned World (J.G.
Ballard)
Set in a future where global warming has
melted the ice caps, this novel explores a
flooded and overheated world where
humanity struggles to survive.

Geoengineering
Ambitious but misguided geoengineering projects meant to combat climate change go awry, causing unforeseen environmental disasters and global instability.

Novel: The Ministry for the Future (Kim Stanley Robinson)
This novel explores various strategies, including geoengineering, aimed at mitigating the effects of climate change in a near-future world and the ethical dilemmas they present.

Movie: Elysium
In this science fiction film, geoengineering solutions have been implemented to create a utopian space station for the elite, leaving the Earth below in a state of environmental decay and chaos.

Global Warming
Extreme global warming causes rising sea levels, catastrophic weather events, and the melting of polar ice caps. Habitability becomes a challenge as cities flood and ecosystems collapse.

Movie: The Day After Tomorrow
In this disaster film, abrupt global warming triggers a series of extreme weather events, leading to a new Ice Age and catastrophic consequences for humanity.

Novel: Flight Behavior (Barbara Kingsolver)
This novel centres around a rural community affected by unusual climate-related phenomena, including the migration of monarch butterflies, highlighting the personal and ecological impact of global warming.

Governmental Oppression

An authoritarian regime takes control and uses surveillance, propaganda, and force to suppress dissent, resulting in a dystopian society. They could even enforce Martial Law.

Novel: 1984 (George Orwell)
This classic dystopian novel depicts a totalitarian regime that exerts complete control over its citizens, erasing individuality and free will in a bleak and oppressive future.

Novel: The Hunger Games (Suzanne Collins)
In this young adult dystopian series, a totalitarian government known as the Capitol maintains control by forcing children from the districts to participate in a televised fight to the death.

Loss of Biodiversity

The extinction of key species disrupts ecosystems, causing a chain reaction of ecological collapse and societal disarray.

Movie: Silent Running
In this science fiction film, the last remaining forests and biodiversity of Earth are preserved aboard a spaceship as the planet becomes ecologically devastated.

Movie: Avatar
While primarily a science fiction adventure,
the film explores the themes of biodiversity
loss and environmental destruction as humans
exploit the resources of the alien planet
Pandora.

Loss of Resources

Depletion of vital resources like water, energy, or food triggers conflicts and societal collapse as people fight for survival.

Movie: The Road Warrior
In the post-apocalyptic Australian wasteland,
a cynical drifter agrees to help a small
gasoline-rich community escape a horde of
bandits.

Novel/TV Series: The 100 (Kass
Morgan)
This series is set in a post-apocalyptic world
where nuclear war and environmental
collapse have resulted in the loss of
biodiversity and the degradation of Earth's
ecosystems.

Mass Hysteria or Collective Delusion

A worldwide phenomenon leads to mass hysteria, delusion, or the acceptance of a false reality, resulting in societal breakdown.

Movie: The Happening
In this thriller, an unexplained phenomenon
causes mass hysteria and collective delusion,
leading people to commit acts of self-
destruction.

TV Series: Black Mirror
Several episodes of this anthology series
explore the consequences of collective delusion
and mass hysteria, often driven by the
influence of technology and media.

Mass Migration and Overpopulation
Massive migrations due to war, climate change, or
other factors overwhelm existing societies, leading to
chaos and conflict.

Novel: The Space Between Worlds
(Micaiah Johnson)
In this science fiction novel, overpopulation
and the scarcity of resources have led to a
system where only a select few can travel
between parallel universes, exacerbating
social inequalities.

Novel: Stand on Zanzibar (John
Brunner)
This science fiction novel depicts a world
grappling with overpopulation and mass
migration, resulting in social and political
tensions that threaten global stability.

Memory Loss or Mind Control
A widespread event wipes out memories or subjects
individuals to mind control, leading to a world where
reality is uncertain and controlled by others.

Movie: Eternal Sunshine of the Spotless Mind
While not a traditional world-ending scenario, this film delves into the consequences of memory erasure and its impact on relationships and individual identity.

Novel/Movie: The Giver (Lois Lowry)
In a seemingly utopian society, the protagonist discovers the dark truth about the suppression of memories and emotions, challenging the stability of the world.

New Ice Age
In this scenario, the world plunges into a prolonged and severe ice age, with glaciers covering vast areas. This results in the depletion of resources, mass migrations, and struggles for survival in freezing conditions.

Novel: The Fifth Sacred Thing (Starhawk)
Set in a future San Francisco, the story explores a world threatened by ecological disaster, including the onset of a new ice age, and the struggle between a utopian community and a militaristic regime.

Novel: Dark Eden (Chris Beckett)
The novel takes place on a distant planet where the offspring of two stranded astronauts reside in eternal darkness, confronting environmental obstacles reminiscent of a new ice age.

Nuclear Warfare

A large-scale nuclear conflict results in a devastated world with radiation, scarce resources, and societal breakdown.

TV Series: Jericho
This post-apocalyptic series depicts the aftermath of nuclear attacks on major U.S. cities and the struggles of a small town to survive, including the threat of chemical weapons.

Movie: The Day After
This 1983 television film portrays the immediate aftermath of a nuclear war, including the effects of an EMP on electronic devices and communication systems.

Pandemic or Disease Outbreak

A deadly virus spreads rapidly, causing widespread illness and death, disrupting societies, and leaving survivors in a post-apocalyptic world.

Novel/Movie/Limited Series: The Stand (Stephen King)
A super flu wipes out most of the world's population, and survivors are drawn to two opposing leaders, setting the stage for a battle between good and evil.

Novel: Oryx and Crake (Margaret Atwood)
Set in a dystopian future, the novel explores a genetically engineered pandemic and its impact on society, nature, and morality.

Plant Diseases

Widespread crop failures due to plant diseases result in food shortages, leading to conflicts over resources and societal instability.

Novel: Seed (Rob Ziegler)
Set in a future where climate change has drastically altered the world, the novel involves a bio-engineered super-plant that becomes a crucial resource in a dystopian landscape.

Novel/Movie/TV Series: The Day of the Triffids (John Wyndham)
While not a traditional plant disease, the novel features aggressive, mobile plants known as Triffids that pose a threat to humanity and contribute to societal collapse.

Poisoned Water

A contamination of water sources, whether through industrial pollution, chemical spills, or biological agents, renders most water undrinkable, causing widespread health crises and social instability.

Novel: The Water Knife (Paolo Bacigalupi)
This novel envisions a future world where water scarcity and contaminated water sources have caused a societal collapse in the American Southwest, leading to resource wars.

TV Series: Z Nation
In this post-apocalyptic series, a zombie virus has contaminated water sources, leading to a world where waterborne infections are a constant threat.

Resource Monopoly
A powerful corporation or entity gains control over essential resources, manipulating societies and creating a world of haves and have-nots.

TV Series: Incorporated
In a dystopian future where corporations have gained unprecedented power. The show follows a junior executive who infiltrates a powerful mega-corporation to uncover the dark secrets behind its control and the oppressive societal divisions it perpetuates. But he has dark secrets of his own.

Movie: Mad Max: Fury Road
In a post-apocalyptic wasteland, a tyrannical warlord controls the scarce resources, particularly water and fuel, leading to a struggle for survival among the remaining inhabitants.

Rise of Supremacist Ideologies
While scenarios involving the rise of supremacist ideologies leading to a dystopian world may not be as prevalent, sometimes such themes are explored.

Extremist ideologies gain dominance, leading to discrimination, oppression, and conflict on a global scale.

Novel: Delirium (Lauren Oliver)
*A world where love is considered a disease,
leading to strict control and suppression of
emotions.*

Movie: V for Vendetta
*In a totalitarian society, a masked vigilante
named V fights against a fascist regime that
promotes supremacist ideologies, aiming to
ignite a revolution.*

Social Unrest

When things get really tough and people are very
unhappy, violence might break out. People might
think they have to hurt others to protect themselves.
This could lead to a lot of fighting, not enough
resources, and a gigantic mess everywhere.

TV Series: 3%
*In a future where only 3% of the population
can live in luxury, the series depicts a
dystopian society marked by social unrest as
candidates undergo a challenging selection
process.*

*Novel: The Dispossessed (Ursula K. Le
Guin)*
*Set on two planets with contrasting political
systems, the novel explores the consequences
of social unrest and rebellion in a society
striving for utopia.*

Solar Event

A powerful solar event, such as a massive solar flare or coronal mass ejection, disrupts electronic systems on Earth, leading to chaos, infrastructure collapse, and communication breakdowns.

Movie: Knowing
A professor discovers a series of mysterious numbers predicting major disasters, including a solar flare that could change life on Earth.

TV Series: Into the Night
Passengers on a hijacked flight try to outrun the sun as it brings deadly solar radiation to the entire Western hemisphere.

Supernatural or Mythical Events

The appearance of supernatural phenomena or mythological creatures disrupts the world's natural order, leading to societal collapse.

Novel: The Darkest Minds (Alexandra Bracken)
A mysterious disease affecting children, resulting in supernatural abilities and government control.

Novel: Enclave (Ann Aguirre)
A post-apocalyptic world with dangerous mutated creatures and a society living underground.

Super Storms (Natural Disaster)
Frequent and intense superstorms, possibly because of climate change or other causes, devastate coastlines and regions, making it difficult for communities to rebuild and survive.

> *Movie: Geostorm*
> *In a near-future where satellites control the climate, a malfunction triggers a series of superstorms, and a team must race against time to prevent a global catastrophe.*
>
> *Movie: Category 6: Day of Destruction*
> *A miniseries depicting the chaos and destruction caused by a series of extreme weather events, including superstorms, as a group of meteorologists races to prevent a catastrophic event.*

Super Volcanoes (Natural Disaster)
The eruption of massive super-volcanoes leads to a volcanic winter, which drastically reduces global temperatures, disrupts agriculture, and causes food shortages.

> *Movie: Dante's Peak*
> *A volcanologist and the mayor of a small town must navigate the threats posed by an awakening super volcano, leading to a tense race for survival.*
>
> *Novel: Ashfall (Mike Mullin)*
> *The novel follows a teenager's journey through a post-apocalyptic landscape, navigating the aftermath of a super volcano eruption that blankets the world in ash.*

Technological Catastrophe

A technological advancement gone wrong, such as artificial intelligence gaining control or a devastating cyberattack, plunges the world into chaos.

Novel: Warcross (Marie Lu)
A society heavily reliant on a virtual reality game, blurring the lines between reality and technology.

Movie: Blade Runner
Set in a future where advanced bioengineered beings, known as replicants, challenge the definition of humanity, the film explores the ethical implications of creating artificial life.

Time Travel Paradox

Time travel experiments go awry, creating paradoxes that alter history and result in a dystopian present.

TV Series: Terra Nova
Set in a future where Earth is overpopulated and polluted, the series follows a family sent back in time to a prehistoric Earth to rebuild civilization.

Novel: The End of Eternity (Isaac Asimov)
In this classic science fiction novel, a secret organization known as Eternity manipulates time to prevent disasters, but their actions have unintended consequences.

Viral Epidemic

However, there is the risk that there could be a virus that mutates and that it results in an epidemic of people dying due to the lack of a vaccine being available to fight it. Outbreaks of deadly diseases, whether natural or engineered, result in high mortality rates, collapse of healthcare systems, and social disintegration.

The Maze Runner (James Dashner)
A mysterious illness called the Flare, turning people into Cranks, and the WICKED organization's experiments.

TV Series: The Last Ship
A naval destroyer becomes one of the last safe places on Earth after a global pandemic wipes out most of the population, and the crew works to find a cure.

Zoonoses

Diseases originating from animals, such as viruses or bacteria, jump to humans, causing pandemics and societal disruption as healthcare systems struggle to respond.

Novel/Tv Series: Zoo (James Patterson)
What happens when the animals start to attack humans? A team comes together and searches to find out what's causing a rash of violent animal attacks.

Tv Series: Dark Angel
In this unique series, a group of genetically
enhanced children, infused with animal DNA,
breaks free from a lab experiment. Flash
forward to a post-apocalyptic Pacific
Northwest, where one escapee, now employed
by a messenger service, plays a central role in
the story.

Summary

Remember, the way the world ends in your dystopian fiction novel can influence the tone, themes, and conflicts of the story. Choose the scenario that best aligns with the message you want to convey and the atmosphere you wish to create.

You can also mix and match your world. For example, we can have a virus that creates vampires who can time travel. Anything is possible.

Before the Apocalypse

Depending on the story you are writing, your characters may have to prep for an imminent world ending event. In a dystopian world, where resources and safety are scarce, it's important to consider what items your characters would need to store to increase their chances of survival and well-being.

Animals and Pets
If applicable, animals for companionship, protection, or help in survival tasks. Plus, food to feed them.

Bartering Items
Items like valuable tools, seeds, or other goods that they could use for trade.

Basic Tools
A multipurpose tool, a knife, a flashlight, batteries, binoculars, flares, matches, lanterns, and other tools for survival tasks.

Books and Educational Materials
Survival guides, medical manuals, and educational resources for acquiring essential skills.

Cash and Precious Metals
A small amount of cash and valuable metals that might hold value in a post-currency world. Jewellery and ornaments.

Cloth and Sewing Supplies
Fabric, thread, and needles for repairing clothes and creating functional items.

Communication Devices
Battery operated radios, walkie-talkies, or other devices to stay connected with others and gather information.

Community and Networking Resources
Building connections with others who can share resources, skills, and support.

Entertainment and Psychological Support
Books, puzzles, games, or other forms of entertainment to maintain mental well-being.

Fire-Making Tools
Lighters, matches, fire-starting kits, and fuel to create warmth, cook food, and provide light.

Fuel and Energy Sources
Portable stoves, fuel canisters, and solar chargers for devices.

Hygiene Supplies
Soap, toothbrushes, toothpaste, feminine hygiene products, baby wipes, and other hygiene essentials.

Medicine and First Aid Supplies
Prescription medications, basic first aid supplies, and medical equipment to address injuries and illnesses.

- ☐ Antibiotic Ointment
- ☐ Aspirin
- ☐ Bandages
- ☐ Burn Cream
- ☐ Eye Wash Solution
- ☐ Gauze
- ☐ Ibuprofen
- ☐ Rubber Gloves
- ☐ Scissors
- ☐ Splint
- ☐ Stitching Kit
- ☐ Thermometer

Non-Perishable Food
Canned foods, dried fruits, nuts, and energy bars to sustain them when food becomes scarce. During the summer months, they may have to dig holes or find an underground basement area where they can keep items cooler.

Personal Identification and Important Documents

Copies of identification, passports, medical records, and other essential documents.

Potassium Iodide tablets

Potassium Iodide pills can be used by everyone in the story if they've been exposed to harmful things like radiation, bad gases, or chemicals. They'll help keep the characters from getting seriously sick by protecting their thyroid glands.

Seeds and Gardening Supplies

Seeds for growing food, gardening tools, and knowledge about cultivating crops.

Self-Defence Items

Pepper spray, self-defence tools, or even basic weapons for protection.

Shelter Materials

Tarps, tents, or materials to build makeshift shelters for protection from the elements. Cots and Sleeping Bags. Anything camping related.

Warm Clothing and Bedding

Warm clothes, blankets, pillows, pup tents, and sleeping bags to stay comfortable in changing weather.

Water and Water Purification Tools

Bottled water or water filters to ensure a clean water supply, which is essential for survival. Better to have too much than not enough.

Summary

Remember, the specific items they store would depend on the dystopian scenario in your story. Flexibility, adaptability, and the ability to improvise will be crucial in surviving the challenges of a dystopian world.

Survival Skills

Characters in a dystopian fiction world would need a range of survival skills to navigate the challenging conditions of their environment. These skills are essential for their safety, well-being, and the ability to thrive in a world filled with threats and uncertainty.

One character would not know everything, but a group of characters might have the skills to survive.

Here are some key survival skills characters might need.

Basic First Aid
Knowing how to treat wounds, injuries, and illnesses is crucial. Characters should be able to clean wounds, apply bandages, and provide immediate care until

professional medical help is available. They need to think outside the box and use the tools on hand.

Basic Mechanics
Understanding how to repair and maintain essential equipment, vehicles, or machinery can be crucial in a world where resources are scarce.

Belief in Yourself
This is the time for your characters to fully believe in themselves 100%. Survival depends on them taking risks, being brave, and going the distance.

Communication Skills
Characters should know how to use communication devices like radios or walkie-talkies, as well as signaling methods like smoke signals or flares.

Crisis Management
Being able to make quick decisions under pressure and stay calm during emergencies is vital for survival.

Fire-Making
Knowing how to start and maintain fires using various methods, such as friction, flint and steel, or fire starters, is essential for warmth, cooking, and signalling.

Growing Food
When your characters are facing an end of the world situation, they need to do what they can to grow their own food. They need to have skills that help them with determining what to plant, how to get the soil ready, watering, harvesting, and keeping predators out of the garden.

Hunting and Foraging
Characters should have a knowledge of local flora and fauna to identify edible plants, hunt small game, and fish for food.

Leadership Skill
If your character is going to be a leader in a crusade to survive, they have to demonstrate trustworthiness to people. They have to be kind, direct, and able to delegate responsibilities.

Martial Arts/Self Defense
The element of surprise may be there when someone or something attacks you if your characters know martial arts.

Learning self-defence techniques, including hand-to-hand combat and the use of improvised weapons, can help characters protect themselves from threats.

Medical Skills
Beyond basic first aid, characters with medical knowledge can treat more serious injuries and illnesses, increasing their group's chances of survival.

Military Training: Part of military training is being able to survive in the most unusual of circumstances. If a character has been in any branch of the military, they have an upper hand with additional survival skills.

Navigation
The ability to read maps, use compasses, and navigate by landmarks or celestial objects can help characters find their way in unfamiliar or changing landscapes.

Negotiation and Diplomacy
Characters may need to negotiate with other survivors or groups for resources or alliances.

Outdoor Survival
There are survivalists who have done their homework, and they are up to the challenge of living in the wild for days, weeks, months, and even years at a stretch with no problems. A character with this skill set would be invaluable in a dystopian world.

Psychological Resilience
Developing mental resilience, coping strategies, and stress management skills can help characters endure the psychological toll of a dystopian world.

Resource Management
Efficiently managing limited resources like food, water, and ammunition is essential for long-term survival. Since you do not know how long you will need to depend on them, you need to make sure resources aren't being wasted. You should definitely store items in different spots.

Scouting and Surveying
Knowing your environment will be a crucial survival skill when your characters are some of the few remaining out there. They will want to take actions in advance to ensure they have an advantage in case of difficulties.

Shelter Building
Characters should be able to construct basic shelters from natural materials or salvage materials from their environment to protect against the elements.

Stealth and Evasion

The ability to move quietly and avoid detection is valuable for avoiding dangerous situations and hostile individuals.

Teamwork and Leadership

Effective collaboration and leadership skills are essential for building and maintaining a supportive community or group.

Trust Your Instincts

Your characters are going to have to make some life-altering decisions, and they can't be second guessing themselves. They must trust their instincts to survive. This can include taking actions they normally would never be engaged in during the normal course of your life as you know it today.

Water Sourcing and Purification

Finding clean water sources and purifying contaminated water is vital to prevent dehydration and waterborne diseases.

Weapon Use

Your characters need to know how to load a gun, to aim it, and to fire it. If the weapon has a scope, they need to know how to use it to get your target. They will want to cherish their ammo, so they need to get their target on the first shot as often as possible. Knowing how to use a bow and arrow and a knife successfully can help your characters survive.

Summary

These survival skills, both practical and psychological, empower characters to adapt, overcome challenges, and make informed decisions as they navigate the perilous landscape of a dystopian world.

CHARACTER

PRIORITIES

In a dystopian world, characters often face numerous challenges and harsh conditions that shape their priorities. While these priorities can vary depending on the specific context and story, some common themes and main priorities of characters in a dystopian world include.

Adaptation and Innovation

Adaptability and innovation are essential as characters must navigate unpredictable challenges and environments. They often need to improvise solutions to unforeseen problems.

Community and Relationships
Many characters seek companionship and build communities for support, safety, and shared resources. Relationships and trust are crucial in a dystopian world.

Finding Purpose
Many characters search for a sense of purpose or meaning in their lives, especially when the world has lost its sense of order and normalcy.

Freedom and Autonomy
The pursuit of personal freedom and autonomy often drives characters to defy oppressive systems and regain control over their lives.

Health and Well-being
Characters prioritize their physical and mental health, dealing with injuries, illnesses, and trauma. They may also seek moments of respite and happiness amidst hardship.

Hope and Belief
Characters may cling to hope and belief in a better future, even when circumstances seem dire. This hope can be a powerful driving force.

Information and Knowledge
Characters often prioritize gaining information about the world, threats, and opportunities. This might include deciphering the past, understanding new technologies, or uncovering hidden truths.

Justice and Redemption
Some characters are motivated by the desire for justice or redemption, seeking to right past wrongs or hold those responsible accountable.

Legacy and Memory
Preserving the memory of the past and ensuring a legacy for future generations can be a priority, as characters strive to ensure that their struggles and sacrifices are not in vain.

Maintaining Humanity
Characters may strive to hold onto their values, ethics, and humanity in a dehumanizing world. This includes preserving empathy, compassion, and moral principles.

Resistance and Rebellion
In oppressive dystopian societies, characters may prioritize resistance against authoritarian regimes, working to expose corruption or bring about change.

Resource Acquisition
Securing essential resources such as food, clean water, medicine, and fuel becomes a constant concern. Characters may scavenge, trade, or farm to meet their needs.

Safety and Security
Characters seek safety from physical and societal dangers. This may involve fortifying their shelters, forming alliances with others, or staying hidden from oppressive regimes.

Survival

Above all, characters prioritize their survival. This includes finding food, water, shelter, and protection from threats, whether they be environmental, societal, or individual.

Summary

Characters in dystopian fiction often face complex moral dilemmas and make tough choices as they navigate these priorities in a world that has descended into chaos and oppression. These priorities drive the plot and character development, making dystopian stories interesting and thought-provoking.

ALLIANCES

Think about your work crew in the office. The bosses are in charge, the team players are working hard, and everyone is focused on a shared mission. The team's strengths usually tip the scales over the weaknesses, and that's why group projects often get the gold star for productivity.

But, you know, sometimes there's some drama in the mix. Too many folks vying for the captain's hat, while others grumble that they're shouldering more than their fair share of the load. There are always those who treat it like life or death, and then there are the ones who couldn't care less. It's like a little office soap opera sometimes, isn't it?

In a dystopian world, alliances are key. Your characters need each other to survive and pool their resources.

Alliance Leaders
Leaders or representatives from each party often play a role in formalizing alliances. They negotiate the best terms for their party.

Common Goals and Interests
People built collaboration on shared goals, whether it's securing food, water, clothing, protection, or a safe haven.

Communication
Establishing reliable communication channels within alliances is crucial for sharing information and responding to emerging threats.

Conflict Resolution
Agreed-upon processes for resolving disputes prevent internal conflicts from weakening the alliance.

Demonstrated Capabilities
People join forces with those who have proven their skills in getting resources, defending, or solving problems. Not everybody has experience with everything, but in a group people have more skills.

Emergency Alliances
Some alliances may form out of necessity during emergencies, such as facing a sudden attack or disaster. These alliances could fall apart once the danger is gone.

Geographical Proximity
Proximity can lead to natural alliances, because groups or individuals that are near each other are more likely to work together.

Inner Conflict

The risk of inner conflict can occur because of differences in opinion, stress, and mental anguish. Some characters just don't do well at all with turmoil, and they may become mean, make mistakes, or become aggressive when their behaviour was never that way before the end of the world event occurred.

Isolation

Humans aren't meant to be alone. Remember that part in I Am Legend with Will Smith? It's like etched in my brain. He was on the edge, craving some human connection so badly that he's there, having a heart-to-heart with a mannequin in a store. That's the level of isolation that can mess with a character's head.

Long-Term Planning

If characters work together and think ahead, they can create societies that will last and give us what we need.

Medical Attention

By creating alliances, characters won't be alone and that can be important for your physical well-being. If they become ill or break a bone, it would be easier for someone else to do it for you.

Mutual Benefit

Characters enter alliances when they believe they can benefit from the relationship. This can involve resource-sharing, defence against common threats, or knowledge exchange.

Negotiation

Forming alliances heavily relies on negotiation. The parties talk it out and decide on what's fair and beneficial for both sides.

Protection and Security

In a dangerous dystopian world, individuals and groups may seek alliances to enhance their security. A larger alliance offers better protection against external threats.

Resource Exchange

Allies share things like food, water, meds, and weapons to get what they need.

Threat of Common Enemies

Nothing brings people together like a common enemy. Your chances for survival are going to improve if you are part of a group.

Trust and Reliability

You can't make alliances without trust. You have to know if you can count on the people you're partnering with. Check if they're reliable and trustworthy. Building trust involves engaging in small interactions over time.

Summary

There are several problems with alliances. Inner conflict, viruses can spread, you need more food for bigger groups, and not everyone will be trustworthy.

Making friends is tricky - you need to weigh the pros and cons, build trust, and have common goals. When survival is tough, these alliances can mean the difference between thriving or not.

Enemies and Antagonists

In dystopian fiction, various entities and groups can serve as potential enemies or antagonists, each contributing to the oppressive and challenging nature of the world. Here's an overview of each of these potential enemies.

AI (Artificial Intelligence)
AI can be a formidable antagonist in dystopian worlds, especially when it gains autonomy and control. It may enforce strict rules, surveillance, and automation, eroding human freedoms and privacy.

Aliens

In some dystopian settings, characters confront mutant creatures, extraterrestrial beings, or otherworldly forces that pose physical threats and endanger their survival.

Corporations

Powerful and unscrupulous corporations can become antagonists when they prioritize profit over human well-being. They may exploit resources, manipulate markets, and perpetuate inequality, leading to societal unrest.

Corrupt Authorities

Characters may contend with corrupt leaders, officials, or law enforcement agencies that abuse their power for personal gain and maintain control through force and manipulation.

Cults

Characters may confront the manipulation of information and propaganda, which can shape beliefs and control the thoughts of the population.

Elders

In some dystopian societies, an older generation can act as antagonists when they hold on to power and restrict the rights and opportunities of younger generations, stifling progress and change.

Environmental Catastrophes

Natural disasters, ecological collapse, and environmental hazards can be relentless enemies, leading to resource depletion and habitat destruction.

Epidemics and Disease
Outbreaks of deadly diseases or pandemics can spread quickly in dystopian settings, threatening character's health and causing chaos.

Factions and Rival Groups
In divided societies, rival factions or groups with conflicting ideologies can become enemies. These factions may compete for resources, territory, or control.

Foreign Citizens
In a world divided by nationalism and xenophobia, people can portray foreign citizens as antagonists when they perceive them as threats or competitors for resources and opportunities.

Government
Government entities, particularly authoritarian or totalitarian regimes, are common antagonists. They use control, propaganda, and repression to maintain power and suppress dissent. They can also use advanced surveillance systems and technology.

Mental Threats
To survive, your character's mind has to be strong and focused. Being alert despite their body feeling fatigue and pushed to its limits is important.

Creativity
Thinking outside of the box is going to be an impressive skill for characters. Getting creative is what they need to do as a common solutions may not work for a scenario.

Loss of Identity

Losing individuality and the struggle to maintain one's identity in a conformist society can be an internal enemy, leading to inner conflicts.

Fear and Despair

Psychological enemies like fear, hopelessness, and despair can erode characters' resilience and motivation.

Moral Ambiguity

Characters might grapple with moral dilemmas and ethical conflicts, where the line between right and wrong becomes blurred in a desperate world.

Isolation and Loneliness

Characters may face the enemy of isolation, leading to loneliness, mental health challenges, and a longing for human connection.

Positive Mindset

When your characters have a positive mindset, they will look for solutions at every turn. They won't let what is a challenge stop them from moving forward with their survival plans. That is often what makes the difference between those that give it their all and those that give up.

Stress

Characters can't allow stress or anxiety to get the best of them. Of course, this is easier said than done when you are seeing mass destruction all around you.

Survivors Guilt
Characters can also wrestle with survivor's guilt from time to time. This is the feelings of regret and sadness that they survived while others didn't.

Time and Aging
The relentless passage of time and the challenges of aging can be subtle yet formidable enemies as characters grapple with mortality.

Military
The military, especially when it becomes a tool of an oppressive government, can act as an antagonist. It enforces the regime's will through force, intimidation, and martial law.

Physical Threats
Characters often face physical threats such as hunger, thirst, exposure to extreme weather, and dangerous wildlife. The scarcity of resources and a harsh environment can be formidable enemies.

Society
The very fabric of society itself can be an antagonist when it enforces strict norms, conformity, and dehumanization. Characters may struggle against societal pressures to keep their individuality and values.

Traitors and Betrayal
Characters may encounter betrayal from within their own groups or communities, as individuals compromise the safety and trust of others.

Summary

These potential enemies and antagonists in dystopian fiction contribute to the complexities and conflicts of the narrative. They challenge characters' beliefs, resilience, and determination, often driving the central themes of resistance, survival, and the human spirit's endurance in the face of adversity.

COMMUNICATION

METHODS

Communication methods would likely be limited and adapted to the challenging circumstances of the world you are creating. Here are a few methods that could be prevalent.

Animal Communication
Some societies might train animals to carry messages, like trained dogs or even carrier pigeons.

Community Bulletin Boards
Characters could use physical bulletin boards in central areas to share important information within a community. They could pin coded messages that only some people could decipher.

Drum or Horn Signals
They might use drumbeats or horn sounds as a form of coded communication, conveying messages through rhythm and pattern. They can also serve as a warning for intruders.

Flares
Flares can light up the sky with bright colours, serving as a signal when words can't be heard. Shooting up a flare can be a way to call for help or let others know where you are, cutting through the darkness with a message of hope.

Graffiti and Wall Messages
People might leave messages on walls or buildings using graffiti or other forms of visual representation.

Handwritten Letters and Notes
In a world without reliable technology, handwritten letters and notes could become the primary means of long-distance communication.

Hidden Messages in Public Spaces
People might leave messages in hidden places for others to find, allowing them to communicate discreetly.

Message Carvings and Symbols
They could leave carvings, markings, or symbols in specific locations to communicate with those who know how to interpret them.

Messenger Runners
People might rely on runners or messengers to physically carry messages between distant locations.

Morse Code or Tap Code
Simple codes like Morse code or tap code could work for covert communication between individuals. For Morse code to work, both parties need to be familiar with it.

Personal Signatures or Symbols
People might develop personal symbols or marks that others recognize as their identity or message.

Radio
It's a good idea to have a radio that runs on batteries. Or an even better idea is to have a radio that you can power by cranking a handle. It's important to have a radio so you won't feel you're all alone in the world.

Radio Broadcasting (Limited)
If some remnants of technology remain, radio broadcasts might be possible, though on a smaller scale and with a limited range.

Signal Flags and Semaphore
Visual communication using flags or semaphore are perfect for short-distance messaging, especially in areas with line of sight.

Smoke Signals
Smoke signals could convey simple messages over long distances, especially in open terrains.

Walkie Talkie
Using a walkie-talkie is like having your own private line of communication. With a push of a button, you can talk to others who have another walkie-talkie, even from a distance. It's a way to stay connected when other forms of communication might not be

working. They don't have the best radius for a signal. However, they can be a valuable tool for scouting, for surveying, and even for keeping watch.

Whisper Networks
Small, tight-knit communities might use word of mouth to spread information within their network, allowing messages to travel quickly.

Summary
When the traditional ways of communicating are gone, people will have to get creative to share information.

FOOD AND WATER

SOURCES

In a dystopian fiction novel, getting food and water can be a daily struggle because of scarcity and adverse conditions. Here are some ways people might secure these essential resources.

FOOD SOURCES

When you are facing physical and emotional stress, eating right is very important.

Agriculture

Characters might cultivate small gardens or farms, growing crops like vegetables, grains, or fruits in hidden locations.

Barter and Trade

Characters might trade valuable items or services for food with other survivors or groups.

Community Resources

Some communities might establish communal kitchens or food distribution centers to ensure fair access to food.

Food Storage

Characters could preserve food through drying, canning, or pickling, extending its shelf life.

Foraging

Characters may gather edible plants, berries, nuts, and mushrooms from the wild to supplement their diet.

Hunting and Fishing

Those with hunting or fishing skills might capture animals or catch fish for food. Organized groups might venture into dangerous territories to secure larger sources of meat or supplies. Weapons can include guns, bow and arrows, traps, and snares.

MRE's

MRE stands for Meals Ready to Eat, and they are very common in the military branches.

Scavenging
Exploring abandoned homes, stores, and warehouses for non-perishable food items can provide temporary relief.

Vegetable Garden
Your characters may create a vegetable garden depending on the climate, soil and water conditions.

Note: Your characters will also have to consider how to dispose of rotten food items and protect their food supply from prowling animals and other humans.

WATER SOURCES

The body can't go long without water, so that is the most essential item for survival. Yet not all water is going to be clean enough to drink.

Condensation
Some characters might use condensation techniques, such as solar stills, to extract moisture from the air.

Desalination
In coastal areas, characters might have access to equipment for desalinating seawater into freshwater.

Dig for Water
If your characters can't find water on the surface, they may need to dig for it.

Foraging

Characters may search abandoned houses, stores etc. for bottles of water. Water will not spoil so this is a commodity you can store for a very long time.

Morning Dew

In the mornings, trees may collect lots of dew. Of course it will depend on the location and the climate for that time of year in your setting.

Purify Water

Characters could boil water for 2 minutes to remove impurities. Or scavenge for water purification drops or tablets to purify the water. They could also add a bit of bleach to their water.

Rainwater Collection

Characters could collect rainwater in containers or makeshift reservoirs for drinking and cooking.

Trade for Water

Bartering with valuable goods or services could secure access to clean water from others.

Water Filtration

Personal water filtration devices or improvised filters might purify available water sources, like rivers or streams.

Water Sharing

Communities might establish water-sharing agreements to ensure fair distribution and conservation.

Wells and Springs

Access to natural springs or functioning wells would be highly valuable and defended resources.

Summary

Survival in a dystopian world often revolves around resourcefulness, adaptability, and community cooperation. Characters may need to innovate and take risks to ensure they have enough food and clean water to sustain themselves in harsh and unpredictable environments.

SHELTER

In a dystopian fiction novel, people would adapt their shelter to the challenging environment and limited resources. Finding shelter on the go is going to be very important. Here are some types of shelter that you can use in your world.

Abandoned Buildings
People might occupy and fortify abandoned buildings for shelter, repurposing them to withstand the elements and potential threats. Department stores would also have supplied.

Agricultural Structures
Characters could convert barns, sheds, and greenhouses into living spaces, offering shelter with resources.

Bunker-like Structures
Underground bunkers, basements, or reinforced shelters might provide safety from threats and environmental hazards.

Caves and Natural Shelters
Natural formations like caves or overhangs make great shelters, offering some protection with no construction needed. Make sure it isn't home to some type of wild creature, though, that is going to become aggressive if you are in their territory.

Community Fortifications
Communities might construct walls, fences, and barricades to create fortified safe zones against external threats.

Cooperative Housing
People might share larger buildings or structures, pooling resources, and skills for collective shelter.

Dry Ditch
One of the simple places for shelter is a dry ditch because it offers you a lower place to protect you from the wind and other elements. Being in a ditch can also help you remain well hidden from other people.

Emergency Shelter Centres
A football field or other extensive public areas are great for emergency shelter centres. It all depends on where your characters are and what type of disaster has occurred.

Fallout Shelter

There are still fallout shelters that were built in the 80s because of the threat of nuclear war. They can be a splendid choice for shelter to get away from chemicals in the air, when the circumstances are unknown, or when there is an epidemic virus going around.

Floating Shelters

In waterlogged or flooded areas, makeshift rafts or floating structures could provide a unique form of shelter.

Hospital

A local hospital has beds, couches, and medical supplies. A hospital is going to have vending machines and a cafeteria where you can find food supplies.

Hunting Blinds

They could repurpose hidden hunting blinds as temporary shelters, offering camouflage and protection.

Large Sized Vehicles

As mentioned previously, they can convert large sized vehicles into a place for shelter.

Lean to/Primitive Huts

Basic huts made from branches, leaves, and natural materials could provide rudimentary shelter in remote areas.

Makeshift Shelters
People might construct simple shelters using salvaged materials like tarps, scrap wood, and debris, providing basic protection from the elements. In a dystopian scenario, they could make shelters from any material that is lying around.

Nomadic Encampments
Mobile encampments like caravans or vehicles changed for living could allow people to move with resources and avoid threats.

School
Schools have ample resting spots because of their vastness. The classroom offers the option to lock the door and ensure safety. The school cafeteria may also have some very large sized cans of food.

Snow Shelters
In icy regions, igloos or snow caves might be used for insulation and protection from extreme cold.

Subterranean Dwellings
Underground dugouts or burrow-like structures could offer concealed shelter from threats and harsh weather.

Tents and Lean-tos
Tents or lean-tos made from cloth, canvas, or other available fabrics could offer portable shelter options. Pup tents set up in a matter of minutes and they are easy to take down (so you can keep moving if necessary).

Treehouses
Elevated treehouses could offer protection from
wildlife and other ground-level dangers, as well as a
vantage point for surveillance.

Summary
The landscape, climate, available materials, and the
need for security against threats both human, animal,
and environmental would influence shelter options.
Adaptability and resourcefulness would be key in
creating safe havens for survival.

Energy Options

Because resources are scarce and your characters need to survive, it'll likely narrow down the options for non-traditional energy. How is your world going to be prepared for creating energy during an end of the world scenario?

Here are some energy options that might work for your story:

Animal Power
In agricultural settings, animals could power simple machines like grain mills or pumps. You can also use them to pull a plow or gardening tools.

Battery Storage (Limited)
Batteries salvaged from the old world might store energy generated from various sources, offering intermittent power.

Biogas Generation
Your community could harness decomposing organic matter to generate biogas, providing fuel for cooking and heating.

Candlelight and Oil Lamps
Simple candles and oil lamps could provide light and a small amount of heat, especially during the night.

Chemical Reactions
They might harness chemical reactions like those used in basic batteries to generate limited electrical power.

Community Energy Sharing
Small communities might pool their resources to generate energy together, sharing the benefits and challenges.

Firewood and Biomass
Burning firewood, leaves, and other biomass materials for heat and cooking would be a common way to harness energy. Your characters will need to make sure they have a safe place to build a fire, though, because a fire that gets out of control can create more problems that affect their chances of survival.

Generator
In a world where power is scarce, a generator becomes a lifeline of energy. With its mechanical heart, it transforms motion into electricity, providing a precious source of power for essential devices and offering a glimmer of modern convenience in a challenging dystopian reality.

Geothermal Heat
In regions with geothermal activity, harnessing underground heat could provide warmth for living spaces.

Hand-Crank Generators
Hand-crank generators could generate electricity by turning a handle, providing a small but essential source of power.

Hydropower (Limited)
If your community lives near water sources, makeshift water wheels or turbines could generate electricity from flowing water.

Kinetic Energy Harvesting
Devices that capture energy from human movement or mechanical actions could power small devices or lights.

Ice and Snow
To offer some refrigeration, you can rely on ice and snow during the colder temperatures. It really depends on the climate where they live regarding what they can count on throughout the year for survival.

Mechanical Energy Conversion
People might convert mechanical movement into energy, such as pedaling to generate electricity for basic devices.

Nuclear Power (Rare)
In advanced settings, remnants of nuclear technology could provide a highly dangerous but potent energy source.

Solar Power
If technology allows, solar panels could generate
electricity from sunlight, providing a renewable
energy source. Solar energy can also recharge some
types of batteries.

Wind Power (Limited)
In areas with strong winds, wind turbines could
provide a limited source of electricity, though
maintenance might be a challenge.

Summary
In a dystopian world, energy would be like gold, and
characters would have to get creative to power their
lives.

Transportation Methods

In a post apocalyptic world, transportation methods would likely reflect the challenges and limitations of the world depicted. Cars, trucks, and motorcycles may or may not exist. And remember that finding fuel might become a big deal.

Here are some transportation methods that could work for your story:

Agricultural Machinery Conversion
Farming equipment like tractors might be retrofitted for transportation, serving as makeshift vehicles for longer journeys.

Airships and Balloons

If technology allows, airships or hot air balloons might provide a means of travel above ground, offering a unique perspective on the dystopian landscape.

Animal-Drawn Sleds

In icy or snowy environments, sleds pulled by dogs or other animals could be used for transportation. In warmer environments, they could adapt sleds with wheels.

Boats, Canoes, Rafts, and Rowboats

In post-apocalyptic scenarios with flooded areas or abandoned cities, water transportation through canoes and rowboats could become essential.

Cars, Trucks, Vans

A personal vehicle is going to be the most common choice. A pickup truck will clear areas where a car may get stuck.

Delivery or Semi-Trucks

A semi truck can be helpful because it's strong, has extra space, and some even have a bed in the front part. Delivery trucks don't have many windows in the back, and they are heavy. They can provide you with a strong framework for creating a reinforced vehicle successfully.

Plus, with the extra room it offers, they can convert part of it as a shelter area. But the problem is, these trucks use a lot of diesel fuel, which is not so good when gas stations aren't operating.

Heavy Machinery
Even though they move slowly, these heavy machines could help you move around. If there's a lot of damage, like trees or poles, in the way, these machines can handle the job of removing them. You can use them to get to a safe spot, and from there, find another vehicle to continue your journey.

Horse-Drawn Vehicles
In a world without reliable fuel sources, you can use horse-drawn carts and wagons for transportation of goods and people.

Human-Powered Transportation
Pedal-powered vehicles, hand-cranked carts, and other human-powered modes of transportation could be used, but they will rely on human resources for mobility.

Mechanical Exoskeletons
In advanced dystopian settings, specialized suits or exoskeletons could enhance human strength and mobility, aiding in long journeys or dangerous terrain.

Military Vehicles
Abandoned military vehicles would provide a wonderful method of transportation. These vehicles were built tough and could provide a sense of security. Police and prison vehicles would also be good choices.

Motorcycles or Scooters
A motorbike or scooter can also be a good way to travel. It uses very little fuel, which is a good thing. You can also use it to easily get around things like stuck cars or fallen trees.

Nomadic Caravans
People might form nomadic caravans of interconnected vehicles, creating mobile communities that traverse the wasteland together.

Plane or Helicopter
Access to a small plane can help people get away from harm and to another destination in very little time. However, very few people have the luxury of such transportation at their fingertips. Issues such as fuel and even monitoring in air space locations though can be reasons not to do so.

Reinforced Vehicle
Depending on the situation, you may not feel completely safe in a common car or pickup. You may need to do some reinforcements with wood, metal, or steel around it. You may need to create some type of cage around it to keep others out.

Renewable Energy Vehicles
If societies have harnessed renewable energy, vehicles powered by solar, wind, or other sustainable sources could exist, providing a limited form of modern transportation.

Scavenged Vehicles
Characters might salvage and repurpose abandoned vehicles, cobbling together functional transport from the remnants of the old world.

Steam-Powered Vehicles
Dystopian worlds might repurpose old technologies, like steam engines, for transportation. Steam-powered trains, boats, and even cars could be adapted to become steam powered.

Travel on Footpaths and Rails
Existing footpaths, roads, and railway lines could become important transportation routes, even if vehicles are limited. People might adapt old rail carts for travel.

Underground Transportation
Underground tunnels abandoned subway systems, or makeshift tunnels might offer a secretive means of travel and evasion.

Walking and Bicycles
With fuel scarcity and limited resources, walking and bicycles become essential modes of transportation for short distances. People need to rely on their own physical power to move around.

Summary
Remember that transportation methods would likely be shaped by the scarcity of resources, the need for self-sufficiency, and the adaptations people make to survive in their harsh environments.

At first, these transportation choices might seem good, but if the fuel runs out, they might have to switch to another way of getting around.

When the world is ending, it is every person for themselves. This means taking what you need to survive... even if you don't own it or have legal access to it prior to that point in time.

WEAPONS

Characters would likely use a bunch of different weapons to defend themselves to get through the dangers of their world... like animal or human attacks. It's important for people to have weapons they know how to use to survive, but often they must adapt to the weapons on hand.

Weapons can also help them hunt for food or protect their supplies from others. Here are some weapons that you can consider for your story:

Animals
Characters can train animals to use as weapons or to provide security.

Bows and Crossbows
Silent and deadly, bows and crossbows could provide ranged options for hunting and defence if there is no ammunition.

Chemical
In dire circumstances, chemicals can turn into powerful weapons. Mixing and releasing certain substances can cause harm or even incapacitate enemies. While dangerous, their strategic use can tip the balance in a life-or-death struggle, making them a grim tool in a dystopian world.

Community-Based Defence
Communities might organize defence groups with various weapons and strategies, pooling resources for protection.

Explosive Devices (Rare)
In advanced dystopian settings, individuals might possess or create crude explosive devices for tactical use. They can even open doors to get into a store or other locked vicinity should you need additional supplies, and all laws have gone out the window. You don't see explosives like grenades or homemade bombs very often because the supplies are scarce.

Firearms (Limited)
If ammunition is scarce, firearms like handguns, shotguns, and rifles might still be used sparingly for their intimidation and defensive capabilities. Any of these types of guns can help with safety.

Hand-to-Hand Combat Skills
Training in hand-to-hand combat techniques could be an essential skill, allowing individuals to defend themselves without relying on weapons.

Improvised Weapons
People might craft weapons from scavenged materials, creating unique devices to suit their specific needs. Improvised weapons like pipes, wrenches, spears, staffs, and other tools for self-defence.

Knives and Combat Weapons
Knives, machetes, clubs, and improvised weapons like metal pipes or baseball bats could be common choices for close-quarters combat. Knives can also help with cutting ropes, carving, and creating sharp sticks or shanks that your characters can use for additional weapons.

Mounted Weapons
In fortified communities, mounted weapons, like crossbows or even cannons, would provide a means for defence.

Poison and Toxins
Some might resort to using poison or toxins to coat weapons or set traps, exploiting natural resources for lethal effect.

Shield and Defensive Gear
Shields, body armour, and protective gear could offer an advantage in close combat scenarios.

Silenced Weapon
For stealth and surprise, silenced firearms or improvised silent weapons could eliminate threats discreetly.

Slingshots
Simple yet powerful slingshots could launch projectiles with accuracy, serving as a versatile weapon.

Swords and Axes
Those with training might use traditional weapons like swords and axes, offering effective tools for combat. They could even teach others.

Throwing Weapons
Throwing knives, tomahawks, or even rocks could serve as weapons for surprise attacks or ranged combat.

Traps and Snares
They could set ingenious traps and snares to capture or injure potential threats, providing a form of passive defence. With the use of snares and traps, they will get food while also keeping people away.

Sport Equipment
Some characters use baseball bats, hockey sticks, tennis rackets or other sports equipment as weapons.

Summary
Weapons in a dystopian world would reflect the challenges and dynamics of survival, with individuals and groups adapting to their environment to ensure their safety and well-being.

Clean Air

We take many things that our bodies engage in for granted, including breathing. Yet it can become a key to survival if there is a catastrophic event that unfolds. Being able to get access to clean air may make the difference between life and death.

Clean air may be scarce in a dystopian world, given environmental pollution, disasters, or other challenges. People would need to employ various methods to ensure access to breathable air.

Air Filtration Systems
If they want to breathe clean air, they might need an advanced air filter. If power still exists, use air conditioners and fans to keep the air circulating in the shelter.

Air Quality Alerts
If the air quality gets worse, sensors and alarms can tell you to take cover or turn on your air purifier.

Air Supply Runs
People in the community could get together and collect air purification equipment or oxygen tanks from deserted buildings.

Biological Solutions
They could use genetically engineered plants or algae to clean up the air.

Controlled Environments
It's possible for communities to create controlled environments in sealed structures with carefully monitored air quality.

Environmental Hazmat Suits
Hazmat suits designed to protect against hazardous materials might create a barrier between individuals and polluted environments.

Facial Masks
Facial masks can help to prevent harmful elements from being part of the air your characters breathe. There can be lots of dust settling for days or weeks after a natural disaster.

Gas Masks and Respirators
Gas masks and personal respirators would be crucial for venturing into contaminated areas or protecting oneself from harmful airborne substances.

Renewable Energy Sources
Communities might use renewable energy sources like solar or wind power to operate air filtration systems and maintain air quality.

Scavenging for Clean Air
Characters might embark on journeys to find pockets of clean air or regions less affected by pollution or contamination.

Secure an Area
Securing your living space is crucial in a dystopian world. If your character is living in a large space, consider using plastic and duct tape to seal off unused areas. Secure windows and doors to help prevent contamination from entering.

Survival Education
Characters might learn survival skills, like checking and improving air quality in makeshift shelters.

Underground Bunkers
Some people could seek refuge in underground bunkers or shelters designed to protect against airborne contaminants. These spaces might have their air purification systems.

Summary
The availability of breathable air is crucial for survival in a dystopian world where clean air is scarce. The characters would have to be resourceful and use technology and knowledge to ensure access to the cleanest air possible.

MEDICAL

EMERGENCIES

In a dystopian fictional world where access to medical care is limited or nonexistent, characters may need to rely on basic medical knowledge, improvisation, and ingenuity to deal with various medical emergencies. Here are some ways characters could address medical issues in such a world.

CONVENTIONAL HEALING METHODS

Allergic Reactions
- Using natural antihistamines like certain plant extracts.
- Administering an epinephrine auto-injector if available.

Bites and Stings
While not usually causing death. Bites and stings can be problematic.
- Cleanse the affected area with soap and water or an antiseptic, if available.
- Applying a cold compress to reduce pain and swelling.
- Using natural remedies like crushed herbs or plant extracts for pain relief.

Broken Bones and Dislocations
A compound fracture involves the bone sticking out through the skin. A closed fracture is one where the broken bone hasn't punctured through the skin.
- Creating makeshift splints from branches, boards, or other rigid materials.
- Applying ice to any type of break can help to reduce the pain
- Wrapping the splint around the injured area to immobilize it
- Using strips of fabric or cloth to secure the splint in place.

Burns

The area around a burn is going to swell so you want to remove clothing from the burned area immediately.

- Cooling the burn with clean water or cold, wet cloths to reduce pain and prevent further damage.
- Applying a sterile bandage or cloth.
- Administering pain relief if available.
- Change the dressing daily and watch for signs of infection.

Childbirth

The thought of giving birth without a doctor around is scary stuff. Yet the truth is that the female body completes the process naturally.

- If a character is pregnant, they may seek help from someone with basic midwifery knowledge.
- Boiling water and sterilizing tools for a makeshift delivery environment.
- Using clean cloths or fabric as improvised birthing aids.
- Assisting with the delivery and ensuring proper hygiene to reduce infection risk.

Choking

- Administering abdominal thrusts (Heimlich maneuver) to dislodge the object obstructing the airway.
- Encouraging coughing and staying with the choking individual until the obstruction is cleared.

Fevers:
- If you have over the counter products such as ibuprofen, you can use them to reduce a high fever.
- If you are in the wilderness, boil some tree bark in water and make a tea out of it. This is a natural remedy to help reduce fever that works quickly.

Infections
- Cleaning and disinfecting wounds to prevent infection.
- Using natural antimicrobial agents like honey or certain plant extracts.
- Monitoring for signs of infection and seeking medical help if necessary.

Poisoning
- Inducing vomiting if appropriate and advised for the type of poisoning.
- Administering activated charcoal, if available, to absorb toxins.
- Providing supportive care, such as fluids and rest.

Respiratory Distress
- Performing basic CPR if someone stops breathing.
- Clearing airway obstructions if choking is suspected.
- Administering rescue breaths and chest compressions.

Stitches

If a cut or a puncture is ¼ of an inch deep or more, then stitches are a good idea for closing the cut.

- Using sterilized thread or fishing line and a curved needle for basic suturing.
- Cleaning wounds thoroughly with boiled water or alcohol.
- Applying a sterilized bandage or cloth afterward.
- Super glue can be used in a pinch if you don't have supplies for stiches.
- Stitches need to be done soon after the cut or puncture or they won't be any good.

Wounds from Weapons

- Cleaning the wound with sterilized water or alcohol, if available.
- Applying pressure to control bleeding.
- Using clean fabric or clothing as bandages or dressings.

In a dystopian world, characters often have to make do with limited resources and medical knowledge. Improvisation, resourcefulness, and basic first aid skills become essential for their survival and the well-being of their community.

Holistic Healing Methods

Many may turn to alternative forms of healing and wellness, often rooted in holistic medicine or what some might call woo woo medicine.

These practices, though often met with skepticism in conventional society, would gain prominence for their perceived effectiveness in alleviating physical and mental ailments.

Healers and Mystics
In this harsh and unforgiving world, healers and mystics are revered for their ancient wisdom and unconventional methods of healing. Holistic medicine, often dismissed as woo by skeptics, encompasses a range of practices, including herbal remedies, energy healing, and spiritual therapies.

Herbalists
Herbalists gather knowledge of local plants and their medicinal properties, concocting potions and salves to treat everything from wounds to respiratory ailments.

Energy healers
Energy healers channel unseen forces to balance the body's energy fields, bringing relief to physical and emotional pain.

Spiritual Guides
And spiritual guides offer solace and guidance, using rituals and ceremonies to help individuals find inner peace and purpose.

Summary
In a world where medical supplies are scarce; these alternative approaches offer a glimmer of hope to those seeking relief from suffering. Skepticism fades as individuals witness the tangible benefits of these unconventional therapies, finding comfort and healing in the unlikeliest of places.

Hygiene

When reality sets in for the end of the world, simple things we take for granted will be gone. Maintaining cleanliness and good hygiene practices is crucial for characters in a dystopian fiction novel to prevent illness, infection, and maintain a sense of well-being, even in challenging circumstances. Here are some ways people in a dystopian world might ensure cleanliness and practice good hygiene:

Basic Sanitation
Establishing designated areas for waste disposal, including human waste, helps prevent contamination and the spread of diseases. People can construct simple latrines or composting toilets.

Bathing
Characters may bathe in natural water sources like rivers or lakes when possible or use limited water resources for sponge baths.

Clothing Maintenance
Characters should take care of their clothing to prevent skin irritations and infections. Regular cleaning and mending are essential.

Disinfection
Using natural disinfectants like alcohol from fermented fruits or homemade herbal solutions can help sterilize surfaces and tools.

Grooming and Hair Care
Basic grooming practices like trimming hair and nails can help prevent discomfort and maintain overall cleanliness.

Handwashing
Emphasizing the importance of frequent handwashing, even with limited resources, helps prevent the spread of diseases. Characters may use water sparingly or make hand sanitizer from ingredients on hand.

Laundry
You can wash clothes using minimal water and homemade detergents.

Oral Care
Maintaining oral hygiene by using toothbrushes and toothpaste, or even chewing on natural alternatives like twigs, can help prevent dental problems. There are various types of plants that can make a paste that will reduce gum inflammation and to reduce dental pain problems.

Personal Hygiene Kits
People could assemble personal hygiene kits containing essentials like soap, toothpaste, toothbrushes, and menstrual hygiene products if available, and use them sparingly to make them last.

Proper Food Handling
Educating characters on safe food handling practices, like cooking meat thoroughly and avoiding cross-contamination, is essential to prevent food-borne illnesses.

Quarantine and Isolation
Characters may implement quarantine measures for the sick to prevent the spread of contagious illnesses. Characters may designate spaces for isolation with limited contact.

Resource Conservation
Emphasizing the need to conserve resources like water and hygiene supplies ensures these essentials are available for an extended period.

Respiratory Hygiene
Promoting practices like covering coughs and sneezes with elbows or tissues and using cloth masks can help reduce the spread of respiratory infections.

Water Purification
Characters may rely on various methods to purify water, such as boiling, using purification tablets, or homemade filtration systems, to ensure access to clean drinking water.

Summary
In a dystopian world, where resources are scarce, practicing good hygiene becomes not only a matter of personal comfort but also a crucial factor in maintaining health and preventing the spread of diseases that could further threaten the community's survival.

CURRENCY

In a post-apocalyptic world, traditional forms of currency like paper money and coins may lose their value or become obsolete because of the breakdown of society and economic systems.

Instead, characters might resort to alternative means of exchange and barter to facilitate trade and gain essential goods and services. Here are some forms of money or exchange mechanisms characters could use.

Agricultural Goods
Food items, seeds, and livestock can be used as currency, especially in agrarian or farming communities where these resources are essential for survival.

Alcohol and Tobacco
These items, if available, can become valuable trade items or currency because of their recreational and medicinal uses.

Ammunition and Weapons
Ammunition and weapons, particularly in a dangerous post-apocalyptic landscape, may be used as currency or traded for other necessities. Be cautious about trading away weapons to people who may turn against you. Ammo or arrows are like gold in this world, and getting your hands on them isn't easy.

Barter System
This is how many people did business back in the days before there was paper money. Bartering is one of the simplest methods of trade, where individuals exchange goods and services directly without a standardized currency.

This could involve trading food for tools, clothing for medical supplies, or any other mutually beneficial exchange.

Cash
The technology we know may be gone, so that means going to the bank to make a withdrawal, driving up to the ATM, or relying on credit or debit cards is out the window.

Community Resources
Some communities might establish their own localized forms of currency, such as tokens or vouchers, backed by shared resources or services within the community.

Favour-Based Economy
In smaller, tight-knit groups, favours and personal debts could become the basis of an informal economy, where individuals help each other with the expectation of reciprocal help in the future.

Fuel and Energy
In a world where resources are scarce, fuel sources like gasoline, propane, or electricity could become valuable commodities used for trade.

Information and Intelligence
Characters with access to valuable information or intelligence, such as maps, survival knowledge, or news about potential threats, may use this as leverage in trade.

Labour and Skills
Skills and expertise in areas like blacksmithing, farming, engineering, or medical care can be offered in exchange for what characters need.

Medicine and Medical Supplies
The demand for life-saving medicines, medical equipment, and first-aid supplies is high, and people will trade them for other goods or services.

Natural Resources
Rare natural resources, like clean water sources, fertile land, or mineral deposits, can become the basis for trade and the establishment of new economies.

Precious Metals and Gems
Precious metals like gold and silver, as well as valuable gems, may serve as currency because of their inherent value and durability.

Scavenged Goods (Theft)

Salvaged or scavenged items from the pre-apocalyptic world, such as books, vintage technology, or historical artifacts, can have value as collectibles or curiosities. All of those rules are out the window in the ultimate quest of survival. You need to take what you need before someone else comes along and gets it.

Summary

In post-apocalyptic settings, the concept of money becomes fluid and adaptable to the specific needs and resources available. Characters may need to be resourceful in determining what has value and how to use it for trade and survival.

Points of Conflict

In a dystopian world, characters could face a wide range of points of conflict, both internal and external, as they strive for survival, security, and a better future. These conflicts add depth and tension to the narrative. Here are some points of conflict that characters might suffer through.

Betrayal and Trust Issues
Characters may grapple with trust issues and betrayal as they try to determine who they can rely on in this uncertain world.

Cultural Clashes
Different survivor groups may have distinct cultures, beliefs, and practices that can lead to misunderstandings and conflicts.

Environmental Hazards
Characters may confront extreme weather, natural disasters, or polluted landscapes that threaten their survival.

Existential Angst
Characters may grapple with existential questions about the meaning of life and the value of their actions in a world where survival is the primary concern.

External Threats
Threats from hostile groups, bandits, or mutated creatures can pose constant dangers and challenges.

Health Crises
Outbreaks of diseases or injuries without access to medical care can create life-or-death situations.

Identity Crisis
The loss of societal norms and roles can cause characters to question their identity and purpose in this new world.

Infiltration and Espionage
Characters might deal with spies or infiltrators from rival groups seeking to gather intelligence or sabotage their efforts.

Loss and Grief
Coping with the loss of loved ones or fellow survivors can be emotionally taxing and lead to inner conflicts.

Moral Dilemmas
Characters might face difficult ethical choices, such as deciding whether to help or harm others for the sake of their own survival or their group's well-being.

Power Struggles
Characters may vie for leadership positions or influence within their community, leading to power struggles and potential divisions.

Quest for Hope
Characters might embark on quests or missions to find a safe haven, discover a cure, or unearth information about what caused the apocalypse, providing a glimmer of hope amid the darkness.

Rebellion and Uprising
Some characters may be dissatisfied with the status quo and seek to overthrow oppressive regimes or leaders.

Resource Scarcity
Competition for limited resources like food, water, shelter, and medical supplies can lead to conflicts within and between groups.

Technological Challenges
In a world where technology may be scarce or malfunctioning, characters may struggle to repair or adapt machinery and devices.

Trauma and PTSD
Experiencing traumatic events can cause post-traumatic stress disorder (PTSD) and affect characters' mental well-being.

Summary

These points of conflict serve not only to test characters' resilience but also to drive the plot forward, making the dystopian world a dynamic and challenging backdrop for their journey.

Quests

In a post-apocalyptic world, quests for survival, meaning, and a better future are common themes for dystopian characters. These quests drive the narrative and offer opportunities for character development and world-building. Here are some quests dystopian characters could embark on.

A Cure
If a pandemic or disease is part of the dystopian world, characters may search for a cure, vaccine, or medical facility to save themselves or humanity.

A Rescue Mission
Saving kidnapped or captured loved ones, allies, or community members from hostile groups or enslavement can be an interesting quest.

Artifacts

Characters might seek valuable or historical artifacts that offer insights into the past and provide hope for the future.

Clean Water

In a polluted or contaminated world, characters might embark on missions to find a pure water source or develop water purification methods.

Discovery of Truth

Characters may investigate the cause of the apocalypse, uncovering secrets and conspiracies that shed light on the world's downfall.

Exploration Forgotten Cities

Venturing into abandoned cities to scavenge supplies, uncover secrets, or confront new challenges.

Exploring the Unknown

Characters may set out to explore uncharted territories or areas previously considered too dangerous, hoping to find hidden resources, allies, or answers.

Hunting for Fuel or Energy Source

In a world where resources are scarce, quests to secure sustainable energy sources, such as solar panels or wind turbines, can be vital.

Hunting for Legendary Items

Tales of legendary items rumoured to possess unique powers can drive characters on epic quests.

Identity
Characters may search for their lost families, friends, or their own pre-apocalyptic identities, grappling with the loss of their former lives.

New Home
Driven from their original settlement, characters may journey to find a new place to call home and start anew.

Reconnection
Characters separated from their group or loved ones may go on quests to reunite with them.

Redemption
Characters burdened by guilt or past actions might embark on a quest to make amends or find redemption.

Resources
Scavenging missions to find essential resources like food, medical supplies, or fuel can be life-or-death quests.

Resistance Against Oppression
Fighting against tyrannical governments, oppressive regimes, or corrupt leaders can be a quest for freedom and justice.

The Recovery of Lost Knowledge
Characters might seek books, archives, or technology repositories to recover lost knowledge and rebuild society.

The Search for a Safe Haven

Characters might journey in search of a secure and fortified location where they can build a new community and protect themselves from external threats.

Unity

Diplomatic missions to form alliances with other survivor groups, fostering cooperation and collective strength.

Summary

These quests not only advance the plot but also provide opportunities for character growth, moral dilemmas, and the exploration of the dystopian world's themes and challenges.

Avoiding Cliches

Avoiding cliches in dystopian stories can make your narrative feel fresh and engaging. Here are some strategies to steer clear of common tropes:

Avoid Tropes
Be aware of common dystopian tropes, such as the chosen one or rebel uprising, and either use them judiciously or find new angles to explore.

Complex Characters
Develop well-rounded characters with depth, flaws, and growth arcs. Avoid one-dimensional heroic rebels or evil overlords.

Cultural Fusion
Blend different cultural elements to create a unique society, avoiding stereotypes or cultural appropriation.

Diverse Perspectives
Include diverse voices, experiences, and cultures in your narrative. Avoid homogenous worlds or token diversity.

Environmental Variation
Dystopian worlds need not be uniformly barren or destroyed. Introduce diverse landscapes and ecosystems that affect characters differently.

Explore Different Themes
Dystopian fiction often revolves around themes like totalitarianism or environmental collapse. Consider exploring lesser-known themes or combining multiple themes in innovative ways.

Explore Unseen Corners
Venture into less-explored aspects of the dystopian world. Instead of the capital city, explore rural communities, remote outposts, or the lives of ordinary citizens.

Innovative Technology
If technology plays a significant role, introduce imaginative and unforeseen advancements or consequences of technology use.

Moral Complexity
Present moral dilemmas and ethical gray areas that force characters and readers to grapple with difficult choices.

Multiple Perspectives
Offer multiple viewpoints within the story. This can provide a richer understanding of the world and its conflicts.

Nuanced Villains
Create antagonists with understandable motivations, complex backgrounds, or shades of gray. Avoid purely evil villains without depth.

Personal Stories
Focus on personal stories and character relationships within the larger dystopian backdrop. Avoid making the dystopia the sole focus at the expense of character development.

Realistic Cause and Effect
Ensure that the dystopian elements have plausible causes and consequences within your world, avoiding overly simplistic explanations.

Subvert Expectations
Challenge conventional storytelling by subverting typical plot twists. Surprise your readers with unexpected outcomes.

Unconventional Narrators
Consider using unconventional narrators, such as non-human or unreliable narrators, to provide a fresh perspective.

Unique Conflict Sources
Deviate from common sources of conflict. Explore interpersonal conflicts, philosophical dilemmas, or moral quandaries that go beyond external threats.

Unique World-Building
Create a distinctive world with its own history, rules, and dynamics. Avoid the temptation to replicate familiar dystopian settings unless you can put a unique spin on them.

Unpredictable Endings

Challenge the expectation of a tidy or purely tragic ending. Leave room for interpretation or open-ended conclusions.

Summary

By thinking critically about your world-building, character development, and thematic exploration, you can craft a dystopian narrative that feels unique, thought-provoking, and memorable.

Novels, Movies and TV Series

Researching (not copying) how others have written can really help you brainstorm. There are tons of dystopian books, movies, and television series. Some like The Handmaids Tale is a novel, movie, and television series.

Novels

1984 (George Orwell)
A Clockwork Orange (Anthony Burgess)
Altered Carbon (Richard K. Morgan)
American War (Omar El Akkad)

Animal Farm (George Orwell)
Anthem (Ayn Rand)
Ashfall (Mike Mullin)
Battle Royale (Koushun Takami)
Beneath a Scarlet Sky (Mark T. Sullivan)
Bird Box (Josh Malerman)
Blindness (José Saramago)
Brave New World (Aldous Huxley)
Cat's Cradle (Kurt Vonnegut)
Dark Eden (Chris Beckett)
Dark Matter (Blake Crouch)
Delirium (Lauren Oliver)
Divergent (Veronica Roth)
Do Androids Dream of Electric Sheep? (Philip K.
Dick)
Dry (Neal Shusterman and Jarrod Shusterman)
Ella Minnow Pea (Mark Dunn)
Enclave (Ann Aguirre)
Fahrenheit 451 (Ray Bradbury)
Fatherland (Robert Harris)
Feed (M.T. Anderson)
Flight Behavior (Barbara Kingsolver))
Genesis (Bernard Beckett)
Good Omens (Neil Gaiman and Terry Pratchett)
Herland (Charlotte Perkins Gilman)
High-Rise (J.G. Ballard)
House of Leaves (Mark Z. Danielewski)
I, Robot (Isaac Asimov)
If on a Winter's Night a Traveler (Italo Calvino)
In the Country of Last Things (Paul Auster)
Johannes Cabal the Necromancer (Jonathan L.
Howard)
Legend (Marie Lu)
Logan's Run (William F. Nolan and George Clayton
Johnson)
Lord of the Flies (William Golding)

MaddAddam (Margaret Atwood)
Make Room! Make Room! (Harry Harrison)
Metamorphosis (Franz Kafka)
Neuromancer (William Gibson)
Metro 2033 (Dmitry Glukhovsky)
Never Let Me Go (Kazuo Ishiguro)
One Second After (William R. Forstchen)
Oryx and Crake (Margaret Atwood)
Parable of the Sower (Octavia E. Butler)
Player Piano (Kurt Vonnegut)
Rainbows End (Vernor Vinge)
Ready Player One (Ernest Cline)
Red Queen (Victoria Aveyard)
Riddley Walker (Russell Hoban)
Scorched (Theresa Shaver)
Scythe (Neal Shusterman)
Seed (Rob Ziegler)
Slaughterhouse-Five (Kurt Vonnegut)
Snow Crash (Neal Stephenson)
Stand on Zanzibar (John Brunner)
Station Eleven (Emily St. John Mandel)
Swan Song (Robert R. McCammon)
The 100 (Kass Morgan)
The 5th Wave (Rick Yancey)
The Andromeda Strain (Michael Crichton)
The Book of Joan (Lidia Yuknavitch)
The Book of the Unnamed Midwife (Meg Elison)
The Children of Men (P.D. James)
The Circle (Dave Eggers)
The Chrysalids (John Wyndham)
The City & the City (China Miéville)
The City and the Stars (Arthur C. Clarke)
The Darkest Minds (Alexandra Bracken)
The Day of the Triffids (John Wyndham)
The Dispossessed (Ursula K. Le Guin)
The Dog Stars (Peter Heller)

The Drowned World (J.G. Ballard)
The End of Eternity (Isaac Asimov)
The Fifth Sacred Thing (Starhawk)
The Fisherman (John Langan)
The Gate to Women's Country (Sheri S. Tepper)
The Giver (Lois Lowry)
The Gone World (Tom Sweterlitsch)
The Hammer of God (Arthur C. Clarke)
The Hand that First Held Mine (Maggie O'Farrell)
The Handmaid's Tale (Margaret Atwood)
The Hitchhiker's Guide to the Galaxy (Douglas Adams)
The Hunger Games (Suzanne Collins)
The Iron Heel (Jack London)
The Knife of Never Letting Go (Patrick Ness)
The Lathe of Heaven (Ursula K. Le Guin)
The Long Walk (Stephen King)
The Left Hand of Darkness (Ursula K. Le Guin)
The Man in the High Castle (Philip K. Dick)
The Man Who Folded Himself (David Gerrold)
The Mandibles: A Family (Lionel Shriver)
The Maze Runner (James Dashner)
The Mezzanine (Nicholson Baker)
The Ministry for the Future (Kim Stanley Robinson)
The Overstory (Richard Powers)
The Plot (Jean Hanff Korelitz)
The Plot Against America (Philip Roth)
The Poisonwood Bible (Barbara Kingsolver)
The Postman (David Brin)
The Penultimate Truth (Philip K. Dick)
The Power (Naomi Alderman)
The Power of the Daleks (Terrance Dicks)
The Raw Shark Texts (Steven Hall)
The Rift (Walter Jon Williams)
The Road (Cormac McCarthy)
The Road to Wigan Pier (George Orwell)

The Rook (Daniel O'Malley)
The Running Man (Stephen King)
The Selection (Kiera Cass)
The Sellout (Paul Beatty)
The Shockwave Rider (John Brunner)
The Space Between Worlds (Micaiah Johnson)
The Stand (Stephen King)
The Trial (Franz Kafka)
The Unincorporated Man (Dani Kollin and Eytan Kollin)
The Wall (John Lanchester)
The Water Knife (Paolo Bacigalupi)
The Wind Through the Keyhole (Stephen King)
The Windup Girl (Paolo Bacigalupi)
The Yiddish Policemen's Union (Michael Chabon)
This Perfect Day (Ira Levin)
Uglies (Scott Westerfeld)
Warcross (Marie Lu)
We (Yevgeny Zamyatin)
When She Woke (Hillary Jordan)
Wool (Hugh Howey)
World Made (Hand (James Howard Kunstler)
World War Z (Max Brooks)
Z for Zachariah(Robert C. O'Brien)
Zone One (Colson Whitehead)
Zoo (James Patterson)

Movies

28 Days Later
A Clockwork Orange
A Scanner Darkly
Akira
Alphaville

Armageddon
Avatar
Blade Runner
Blade Runner 2049
Brazil
Category 6: Day of Destruction
Children of Men
Dante's Peak
Dark City
Deep Impact
Demolition Man
District 9
Divergent
Elysium
Equilibrium
Escape from New York
Eternal Sunshine of the Spotless Mind
Ex Machina
Fahrenheit 451
Gattaca
Geostorm
I Am Legend
I, Robot
Idiocracy
In Time
Incorporated
Independence Day
Interstellar
Into the Night
Knowing
Logan's Run
Looper
Lucifer's Hammer
Mad Max: Fury Road
Metropolis
Minority Report

Outbreak
Planet of the Apes
RoboCop
Rollerball
San Andreas
Silent Running
Snowpiercer
Soylent Green
The 5th Wave
The Book of Eli
The Children of Men
The Day After
The Day After Tomorrow
The Day of the Triffids
The Fifth Element
The Giver
The Handmaid's Tale
The Happening
The Hunger Games
The Island
The Lobster
The Matrix
The Purge
The Road
The Road Warrior
The Running Man
The Stand
The Terminator
They Live
Total Recall
Twelve Monkeys
V for Vendetta
WALL-E
War for the Planet of the Apes
Waterworld
Years and Years

TV Series

3%
Altered Carbon
Battlestar Galactica (2004)
Black Mirror
Black Summer
Brave New World
Children of Men
Colony
Continuum
Counterpart
Dark
Dark Angel
Dark City
Devs
Electric Dreams
Falling Skies
Firefly
Fringe
Gattaca
Humans
Incorporated
Into the Night
Jericho
Minority Report
Mr. Robot
Orphan Black
Person of Interest
Planet of the Apes
Raised by Wolves
Revolution
Salvation
Snowpiercer
Sweet Tooth

Tales from the Loop
The 100
The Expanse
The Handmaid's Tale
The Hot Zone
The Last Ship
The Leftovers
The Man in the High Castle
The Purge (TV series)
The Rain
The Society
The Stand
The Twilight Zone (original and modern versions)
The Walking Dead
The War of the Worlds
Tokyo Vice
Twelve Monkeys
Under the Dome
Utopia
V for Vendetta
War of the Worlds
Westworld
Y: The Last Man
Years and Years
Z Nation
Zoo

CONCLUSION

Congratulations, brave writers! You've now got the basics to embark on your dystopian fiction journey. Start brainstorming. Let your creativity flow and remember that your unique voice is what will make your story stand out.

Explore the depths of dark futures, powerful themes, and unforgettable characters. Your dystopian world is waiting to be born from the ink of your pen. Happy writing!

And there you have it! As we wrap up our journey through the twisting paths of dystopian fiction, remember that the power of this genre lies in its ability to reflect our realities and fears, while also inspiring hope and resilience.

Your own dystopian story is a canvas to explore the what-ifs of society and human nature. As you step away from this guide, take with you the tools, tips, and inspiration we've explored. Let your imagination roam free in the vast landscapes of possibility.

Whether your dystopia is a stark warning or a beacon of hope amidst chaos, your story has the potential to captivate and provoke thought. So, keep questioning, keep imagining, and most importantly, start writing. Your unique voice is what will bring your dystopian world to life. Happy writing!

NEXT STEPS

CHECK OUT MORE WRITING RESOURCES AT

FUNNY FACE FICTION LTD. WE EVEN HAVE

LOTS OF FREEBIES.